F
Meat
Cookery

JOSCELINE DIMBLEBY

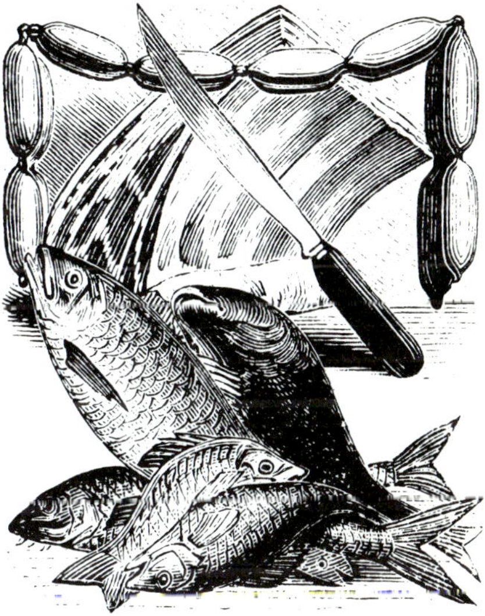

A SAINSBURY COOKBOOK

Published by Woodhead-Faulkner Limited
8 Market Passage, Cambridge CB2 3PF
for J Sainsbury Limited
Stamford House, Stamford Street, London SE1 9LL

First published 1979

ISBN 0 85941 112 5

Cover design and text layout: Ken Vail
Colour photography and cover picture: Bryce Attwell

The publishers wish to thank Elizabeth David, 46 Bourne Street, London SW1, and The Conran Shop, 77–79 Fulham Road, London SW6, for the loan of some of the cookware which appears in the photographs.

Typesetting: Best Typesetting
Printed and bound in Great Britain at
William Clowes & Sons Limited, Beccles and London

Contents

Introduction

> 'All human history attests
> That happiness for man – the hungry sinner –
> Since Eve ate apples, much depends on dinner!'
>
> *Lord Byron*

This is not a book of recipes for the cheapest dishes possible, which would be both limited and uninspiring, but of ideas for making cheaper meat and fish into something more special, so that you can still afford to offer your family a treat or give a dinner party. Providing an exciting and satisfying main course will also save you the added expense and trouble of making a first course. I have tried to show you how to take away the agony of feeling that you have spent too much, so that cooking and entertaining can be a pleasure once more.

Being an incurable bargain hunter I have always found satisfaction and inspiration in creating dishes made from inexpensive ingredients. Inventive cookery does not mean luxurious ingredients – in fact, the most expensive meat and fish are nearly always best cooked in the simplest way. When you use the cheaper cuts, the preparation may take a little more time, but the variety of new and exciting dishes you can create will be both refreshing and rewarding.

If 'cheaper' is something of a relative term when talking about the price of meat, it is even more true of fish. Since fish is much less filling than meat, it is particularly important to make a fish dish more substantial with a good sauce or by mixing it with other ingredients in a delicious fish stew or pie and I have included plenty of recipes of this sort.

I hope this book will help you, both by suggesting new ways of treating old favourites like stewing lamb and minced meat and also by encouraging you to try out unlikely combinations you have never used before. Fillet steak may no longer be within your budget but there are many tempting ways of serving cheaper food which will not only save your pennies but at the same time enhance your reputation as a good cook.

Note: The number of portions is given with each recipe. Most serve four people; where they serve more, it is usually because the dish is more suitable for a larger number of people. However, if you are cooking for only two or three, don't hesitate to reduce the quantities proportionately or divide the finished recipe and freeze some for later. Ingredients are given in both Imperial (oz, pints, etc) and metric (g, ml, etc) measures: use either, *but not a mixture of both*, in any given recipe.

Beef

'And make me savoury meat, such as I love, and bring it to me, that I may eat.'

The Book of Genesis

Beef is the meatiest meat of all and I doubt if real meat eaters will ever be able to do without it. Since we live in a country which has the best beef there is, clear, bright red with rich, creamy-coloured fat, it would be a pity not to make the most of it. Luckily it is a filling meat, so you don't need to buy so much of it, and generally the cheaper cuts have the best flavour.

Look for meat where the fat is evenly distributed, in a marbled effect – beef which is too lean could be tough and tasteless.

French Daube de Boeuf with Olives

Serves 6

Nothing can be much better or more straightforward than the French way of cooking beef and vegetables in a little red wine. No other liquid, and no thickening agent, is used to detract from the delicious, concentrated flavour which the juices acquire after several hours of very slow cooking. It's a simple farmhouse dish which is good enough for any dinner party. An untraditional but, I find, very successful extra touch is to put some soured cream on top of the daube before serving. And, of course, if you can use fresh herbs, so much the better.

1½ lb (600 g) stewing beef, cut into cubes
2 tablespoons (2 × 15 ml spoon) oil
3–4 onions, sliced
¼ lb (100 g) fatty bacon or pork, or a mixture of both, chopped
2 cloves garlic, finely chopped
½ lb (200 g) carrots, sliced thickly
a few slivers of orange rind
2 teaspoons (2 × 5 ml spoon) thyme
2 teaspoons (2 × 5 ml spoon) oregano or marjoram
2 bay leaves
¼ pint (125 ml) red wine
¼ lb (100 g) black olives, stoned and sliced
1 carton (5 fl oz, 125 ml) soured cream (optional)

Heat the oven to Gas Mark 1/275°F/140°C.

Fry the beef all over in the oil to seal it. Transfer to a casserole dish, fry the onions until golden and then add them to the beef, together with the bacon and/or pork, garlic, carrots, orange rind and herbs. Bring the wine to the boil in a small saucepan and set light to it, let the flames subside and then pour it over the meat.

Cover the dish tightly and cook on a low shelf in the oven for 3–3½ hours. Then add the olives and cook for a further half-hour.

Add the soured cream just before serving, just on top – it will mix with the juices as you serve out the daube. Rice, noodles or boiled potatoes all go well with this dish, to soak up the juices.

Ingredients for French Daube de Boeuf with Olives

Oxtail Casserole with Prunes

Serves 6

I think that the rich flavour of oxtail goes best with a sweetish flavour, and prunes give the dish a dark, glossy appearance and an almost sumptuous character. However, if you object to prunes, substitute tomatoes and use ½ pint Guinness instead of the stock.

2 lb (800 g) oxtail
2–3 onions, sliced
¾ pint (375 ml) well-seasoned beef stock
grated rind and juice of 1 orange
5–6 whole cloves
8 oz (200 g) prunes, soaked overnight and then stoned

Fry the oxtail in a little fat until browned all over. Transfer to a casserole dish.

Fry the onions in the remaining fat until brown. Add them to the casserole, together with the grated orange rind and juice, cloves and stock. Cover and put in the oven at Gas Mark 8–9/450–475°F/230–240°C for 20 minutes, until bubbling. Turn the oven down to Gas Mark 1/275°F/140°C, add the prunes and continue cooking for another 2½–3½ hours or until the meat is falling from the bones.

Pour off any excess fat, check for seasoning and serve with boiled potatoes and carrots.

Layered Beef with Cheesy Topping

Serves 4

The combination of meat, tomatoes and cheese is always very successful and the flavour of this simple casserole is hard to beat.

1 lb (400 g) stewing beef
3–4 teaspoons (3–4 × 5 ml spoon) dried oregano
2 cloves, garlic, finely chopped
14 oz (397 g) tin tomatoes
4–6 rashers streaky bacon, with the rind cut off
2 fairly large potatoes
2 large onions, sliced thinly in rings
6 oz (300 g) grated Cheddar cheese
salt, black pepper

Heat oven to Gas Mark 8–9/450–475°F/230–240°C.

If possible, slice the beef in large, thin slices. Arrange half in the bottom of a casserole dish and sprinkle over 1–2 teaspoons (1–2 × 5 ml spoon) oregano, half the chopped garlic, salt and black pepper, and the tomatoes.

Arrange the bacon on top of the tomatoes and then add the remaining beef. Sprinkle with the remaining oregano and garlic, salt and pepper. Peel and slice the potato thinly and add in alternate layers with the onion rings. Finally, top with grated cheese.

Cover the dish and cook in the centre of the oven for 15–20 minutes, then turn down the heat to Gas Mark 1/275°F/140°C for a further 2½–3 hours.

Serve with a green salad or boiled carrots.

Beef and Lentil Flan

Serves 6

Not every flan casing need be made with pastry. Here, a creamy lentil filling is encased by a succulent minced meat mixture and topped with golden cheese.

6 oz (150 g) lentils
1 pint (500 ml) milk
1 onion, finely chopped
$\frac{1}{4}$ whole nutmeg, grated, or $\frac{1}{2}$ teaspoon (2.5 ml spoon) ground nutmeg
1 lb (400 g) fresh minced beef
2 oz (50 g) fresh breadcrumbs
1 level tablespoon (15 ml spoon) tomato purée
1–2 cloves garlic, crushed
2 teaspoons (2 × 5 ml spoon) French mustard
2 eggs, lightly whisked
2–3 oz (50–75 g) grated cheese
salt, black pepper

Put the lentils, milk and onion into a saucepan, bring to the boil, cover and simmer gently, stirring now and then, for $\frac{3}{4}$–1 hour, until you have a thick and mushy mixture. Season with salt, black pepper and the nutmeg.

Season the minced beef with plenty of salt and pepper. Add the breadcrumbs, tomato purée, garlic, mustard and 1 whisked egg.

Heat the oven to Gas Mark 4/350°F/180°C and grease a 9 inch (23 cm) china flan dish. Line the flan dish with the meat mixture, pressing it over the bottom, right up the sides and above the edge. Add the remaining egg to the lentil mixture and spoon it all into the meat casing. Sprinkle the cheese on top. Cook in the centre of the oven for 45–50 minutes until the filling has set. Serve with a tomato sauce and a green salad.

Beef and Lentil Flan

Beef and Mushroom Pie with Cheesy Suet Crust

Serves 4–6

Pies look beautiful and everyone seems to like them. This is a tasty plate pie with a double cheesy crust.

For the filling
1 lb (400 g) minced beef
a little cooking fat or oil
1–2 cloves garlic, chopped finely
1 tablespoon (15 ml spoon) tomato purée
1–2 teaspoons (1–2 × 5 ml spoon) paprika
¼ lb (100 g) mushrooms, sliced
salt, black pepper

For the crust
6 oz (150 g) plain flour
1 teaspoon (5 ml spoon) baking powder
¼ teaspoon (½ × 2.5 ml spoon) salt
2 oz (50 g) fresh white breadcrumbs
2 oz (50 g) grated cheese
4 oz (100 g) shredded suet

Season the mince with salt and black pepper. Melt a little fat in a pan and fry the mince for about 3–4 minutes over a strong heat, stirring with a wooden spoon. Add the garlic, tomato purée and paprika. Remove from the heat and stir in the mushrooms. Check for seasoning and let the mixture cool.

To make the pastry, sift the flour, baking powder and salt into a bowl and stir in the breadcrumbs, cheese and suet. Add enough cold water to form a stiff dough.

Heat the oven to Gas Mark 6/400°F/200°C. Grease a 9–10 inch (27–30 cm) flat pie plate. Divide the pastry in half and roll on a floured board. Shape into two circles big enough for the pie plate. Line the plate with one circle and spoon in the meat filling. Dampen the edges and cover with the other circle. Trim the edges and roll out the trimmings to cut out decorations for the top. Brush with milk and bake in the centre of the oven for 25–30 minutes, until golden brown.

A green vegetable or green salad is all that is needed to accompany this pie.

Lasagne Verde

Serves 6–8

Lasagne takes a little time to prepare but for a family or busy weekend meal it is perfect, as you can make it even a day or two ahead and reheat it. You need only a salad to go with it and I have never known anyone who didn't love it. You can buy the white lasagne if you like, but I prefer the taste and appearance of the spinach-flavoured green variety.

8 oz (200 g) green lasagne
1 tablespoon (15 ml spoon) cooking oil
1 lb (400 g) minced beef
2 tablespoons (2 × 15 ml spoon) tomato purée
2 teaspoons (2 × 5 ml spoon) dried oregano
approx. 2 oz (50 g) butter or margarine
2 oz (50 g) plain flour
1½ pints (750 ml) milk
4 oz (100 g) grated cheese
1 level teaspoon (5 ml spoon) grated nutmeg
a little extra grated cheese or grated parmesan
salt, black pepper

Cook the strips of lasagne in a large open pan of boiling salted water, to which you have added a little cooking oil to stop them sticking together, for 15–20 minutes.

Meanwhile, fry the mince in a large pan with a little oil or fat, stirring it with a wooden spoon to separate it. Add the tomato purée and oregano and season well with salt and pepper. Leave in the pan while you make the sauce.

When the lasagne is soft, drain and rinse thoroughly under cold water.

To make the sauce, melt the butter in a pan, remove from the heat and stir in the flour until smooth. Gradually add the milk. Put back on the heat and bring to the boil, stirring all the time. Let it simmer, still stirring, for about 3 minutes, until it is thick and creamy. Season with salt and pepper and pour about two-thirds of the sauce into the minced meat mixture. Stir the grated cheese and nutmeg into the remaining sauce.

Butter a rectangular ovenproof dish – 10 × 8 inch (25 × 20 cm) or a little larger. Lay pieces of lasagne on the bottom, cutting to shape, then spread over a layer of meat sauce, another layer of lasagne, another of meat sauce and a final layer of lasagne. Pour the cheese sauce over the top, dot with butter or margarine and sprinkle on a little extra grated cheese or parmesan. Heat oven to Gas Mark 6/400°F/200°C and cook just above the centre of the oven for half an hour.

Beef and Bean Hotpot

Serves 5–6

There is something wonderful about the smooth thickness that soaked dried beans give when they are cooked in a stew. I often use them during the holidays when I am feeding crowds of people and need dishes which aren't too much trouble to prepare and which can be kept warm in the oven without spoiling.

$\frac{1}{2}$–$\frac{3}{4}$ lb (200–300 g) dried beans (red kidney, haricot or butter beans)
1–1$\frac{1}{2}$ lb (400–600 g) stewing beef
$\frac{1}{2}$ lb (200 g) smoked streaky bacon, with the rind cut off
a little cooking fat or oil
1 tablespoon (15 ml spoon) plain flour
4–6 cooking tomatoes, chopped roughly
2 onions, peeled and sliced
10 fl oz (250 ml) can beer or equivalent amount of good stock
a sprinkling of Worcestershire sauce (optional)
$\frac{1}{2}$–1 teaspoon ($\frac{1}{2}$–1 × 5 ml spoon) ground nutmeg
2 cloves garlic, crushed
salt, black pepper

Soak the beans in cold water for 8 hours, or overnight. Then boil them in unsalted water until just soft.

Chop the beef into cubes. Cut the bacon in pieces.

Melt enough fat or oil to cover completely the base of a large, heavy saucepan or iron casserole dish. Toss the beef, bacon, beans and onions in the flour, add to pan and cook gently for 2–3 minutes. Add the beer and enough water to just cover the ingredients and stir in the tomatoes. Sprinkle with salt, plenty of black pepper and the Worcestershire sauce.

Bring to the boil and simmer very gently, either on top of the stove (preferably on an asbestos mat) or in the oven at Gas Mark 1/275°F/140°C, for 2$\frac{1}{2}$–3$\frac{1}{2}$ hours, until the beef is meltingly tender.

Pork and Bacon

> 'But since he stood for England,
> And knew what England means,
> Unless you give him bacon
> You must not give him beans.'
>
> *G K Chesterton*

Pork and bacon are often cheaper than other meats but can be very dull and sometimes dry if they are not cooked in an interesting way. Pork is extremely versatile, suitable for both summer and winter dishes. Although the old marriage of pork and apple is certainly a happy one, there is no reason why the apple should be a watery purée.

As with most meat, the more fatty (and therefore the cheaper) cuts of both pork and bacon often have by far the best flavour and texture, hand of pork being a particularly good example.

Pork Steaks with Apple and Spring Onions

Serves 4

This is good enough for a special occasion but still economical, and won't take you long to do. It is, of course, a new version of an old combination of flavours.

4 boneless pork shoulder steaks, 1–1¼ lb (400–500 g) weight
1–2 cloves garlic, crushed
1 dessertspoon (10 ml spoon) chopped fresh or dried rosemary
2–3 oz (50–75 g) butter or margarine
¼ lb (100 g) mushrooms, sliced finely
1 firm eating apple, sliced thinly
1 bunch spring onions, chopped small, using as much of the green stalk as possible
1 wineglass apple juice or sweet cider
salt, black pepper

Rub the steaks with the crushed garlic, sprinkle with salt and pepper and pat on the rosemary. Fry gently in about 1 oz (25 g) of butter, turning once, for 8–10 minutes on each side. Then transfer to a serving dish and keep warm in the oven.

Add another 1 oz (25 g) butter to the pan juices and toss the sliced mushrooms, apple and spring onions over a medium heat for about 2 minutes – not more. Spoon the mixture over the steaks. Then pour the apple juice, seasoned with salt and pepper, into the pan and bubble fiercely over a strong heat for 2–3 minutes, until reduced and slightly thickened. Pour this sauce over the steaks.

Baby carrots and new potatoes are delicious with this dish.

Pork Steaks with Apple and Spring Onions, in preparation

Marrow Stuffed with Pork and Celery

Serves 6

Why is the vegetable marrow so often scorned? Cooked in the right way with interesting seasoning it literally melts in your mouth. Here is my favourite recipe for the homely stuffed marrow.

1 vegetable marrow, about 2½ lb (1 kg) weight
a little butter or margarine
¾ lb (600 g) minced pork (or lamb)
1 oz (25 g) fresh breadcrumbs
2 oz (50 g) grated cheese
3 sticks celery, chopped finely
3 teaspoons (3 × 5 ml spoon) chopped fresh or dried chives
1 egg, beaten
cheese sauce for serving (optional)
salt, black pepper

Peel the marrow, cut in half lengthways and scoop out the seeds. Rub the outside with a little butter. Put both halves on a large piece of foil.

Heat the oven to Gas Mark 4/350°F/180°C. Mix all the other ingredients together thoroughly in a bowl and season well with salt and black pepper. Press the stuffing into both halves of the marrow and join them together again. Wrap up completely in the foil and cook in a roasting pan in the centre of the oven for about 1½ hours, or until the marrow is tender.

This dish is best served with a cheese sauce which you can pour all over the marrow on its serving dish.

Roman Cobbler

Serves 4–5

In our family this recipe is more popular than shepherd's pie, which is saying a lot, and it is not much more trouble to make. The golden top is a cheesy Italian gnocchi mixture and the pork underneath is particularly tasty.

For the topping
¼ whole nutmeg, grated
1 pint (500 ml) milk
4 oz (100 g) fine semolina
3 oz (75 g) grated cheese
1 oz (25 g) butter or margarine
1 egg, lightly whisked
salt, black pepper

For the filling
1¼–1½ lb (500–600 g) boneless pork shoulder steaks
1 oz (25 g) butter or margarine, plus a little more
1 tablespoon (15 ml spoon) oil
2–3 cloves garlic, chopped finely
a small handful of fresh sage leaves, chopped finely, or
  1 teaspoon (5 ml spoon) dried sage
¼ lb (100 g) mushrooms, sliced
a sprinkling of grated parmesan
salt, black pepper

Make the topping at least 2 hours in advance, as follows. Add the nutmeg to the milk in a saucepan, together with salt and black pepper. Stir in the semolina. Bring the milk to the boil and simmer gently for 3–4 minutes until very thick, stirring all the time. Remove from the heat and add the grated cheese, butter and whisked egg. Return to a low heat and stir for a minute more. Oil a large Swiss roll tin or a roasting pan. Spread the mixture evenly over the bottom of the tin. Cover with a cloth and leave to get completely cold – in the fridge if possible.

Using a sharp knife, cut the pork into very small pieces and season with salt and pepper. Melt 1 oz (25 g) butter and the oil in a large frying pan. Stir the pork pieces and chopped garlic over a medium heat for about 5 minutes, until cooked. Add the sage and mushrooms and cook for a further minute or two, stirring the mixture.

Transfer the meat and mushrooms with a slotted spoon into a shallow, ovenproof dish. Bubble the remaining liquid in the pan over a strong heat for a moment or so, until reduced and slightly thickened, and pour over the meat.

Set the grill on medium heat. Cut the cooled topping mixture into fingers (about 2 × 1 inch, 5 × 2.5 cm) and arrange in an overlapping pattern all over the meat. Dot with butter, sprinkle generously with grated parmesan and put under the grill until a rich, golden brown. If necessary, keep the dish hot until needed in a very low oven.

Roman Cobbler

Baked Bacon Joint with Red Beans and Spiced Apples

Serves 6–8

If, like me, you love the flavour of bacon fat you can use the cheapest flank joint for this dish, although, if you prefer, you can use a leaner joint. Either goes very well with the bean and apple mixture and it makes a meal which you can stretch to quite a crowd of greedy people, as you can always cook a few more beans. The meal would be complete with a simple dish of slightly undercooked crisp white cabbage, or just a salad.

8 oz (200 g) dried red kidney beans
$2\frac{1}{2}$–3 lb (1–1.25 kg) boned, rolled bacon joint
about 8 cloves
a few peppercorns
2 oz (50 g) butter or margarine
2 onions, chopped roughly
1–2 cloves garlic, chopped finely
1 large cooking apple
$\frac{1}{2}$–1 level teaspoon (1–2 × 2.5 ml spoon) ground mace or nutmeg
1 tablespoon (15 ml spoon) demerara sugar
$\frac{1}{4}$ pint (125 ml) sweet or dry cider
salt, black pepper

Soak both the beans and the bacon joint in separate bowls of cold water for 8 hours or overnight.

Stick the cloves into the joint and put it into a large saucepan with a few peppercorns. Cover completely with water. Bring to the boil and then gently simmer for 1–$1\frac{1}{4}$ hours.

Meanwhile, boil the beans in unsalted water until soft ($\frac{3}{4}$–1 hour) and drain. Melt the butter in a pan and fry the onions until just soft. Stir in the chopped garlic. Then peel and thinly slice the apple and add to the pan, increasing the heat a little and tossing about for $\frac{1}{2}$–1 minute only – the apple must not go mushy. Stir in the mace and the cooked, drained beans, adding plenty of salt and black pepper. Keep warm in a covered bowl, in a low oven.

When the bacon is ready remove it from the pan and rinse. Heat the oven to Gas Mark 4/350°F/180°C. Remove the string from the bacon and cut or pull the skin from the joint. Score the fat in a diamond pattern and press the demerara sugar on to it. Put the joint into a roasting pan with the cider and cook in the centre of the oven for half an hour or until golden brown, basting now and then with the cider.

Put the joint on a large serving plate surrounded by the beans and apple and pour over any remaining pan juices.

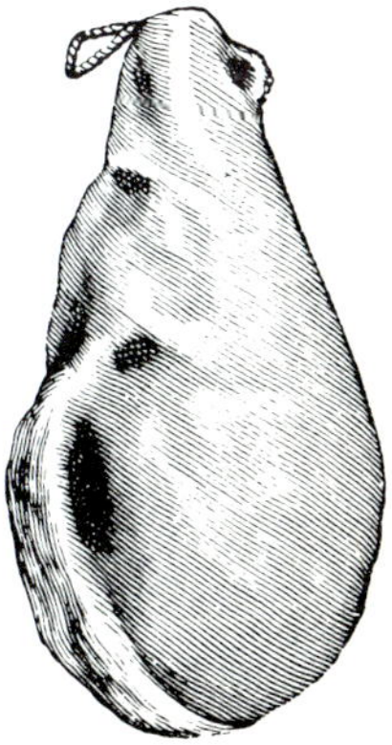

Belly of Pork Chinese Style

Serves 4

This is an excellent way of making the most of an inexpensive cut of meat and producing an exotic dish. The flavour of the root ginger, and its lovely lemony smell, are particularly delicious.

2 large cloves garlic
2 inch (5 cm) piece fresh root ginger or crystallised ginger
1–1½ lb (400–600 g) belly of pork or streaky pork rashers, with the rind cut off
4–5 tablespoons (4–5 × 15 ml spoon) sunflower oil
¾ lb (300 g) white cabbage, sliced very finely
2 teaspoons (2 × 5 ml spoon) sugar
soy sauce
¼ lb (100 g) mushrooms, finely sliced
1–2 oz (25–50 g) flaked almonds
salt, black pepper

Chop the garlic and ginger very finely, mix together and put on one side.

Cut the pork into small pieces and season well with salt and pepper. Heat 2 tablespoons (2 × 15 ml spoon) of the oil in a large frying pan until smoking. Fry the pork over a strong heat, stirring it with a wooden spoon for 10–15 minutes or until golden. Stir in the garlic and ginger mixture and cook for a moment more. Using a slotted spoon, transfer the meat to a serving dish and keep warm.

Add two more tablespoons (2 × 15 ml spoon) of oil to the remaining fat in the pan and add the sliced cabbage. Fry the cabbage in the fat over a strongish heat for 4–5 minutes, stirring all the time. Add salt, black pepper, sugar and several good shakes of soy sauce and cook for a moment more. Stir this cabbage mixture into the meat and keep warm.

Add the remaining tablespoon (15 ml spoon) oil to the pan if necessary, toss the mushrooms and almonds over the heat for only a moment (the mushrooms should not go soft) and then put them on top of the pork. Sprinkle on a little more soy sauce.

Serve with rice and a green salad.

Belly of Pork Chinese Style

Roast Pork with Apple and Walnut Stuffing

Serves 8–10

Taking the trouble to stuff an inexpensive pork joint such as hand, blade bone or even a large piece of belly can transform it into a dish fit for a gourmet.

2½–3½ lb (1–1.3 kg) boned joint of pork
1 large cooking apple
1 squeeze of lemon juice
1 tablespoon (15 ml spoon) sugar
2 oz (50 g) fresh brown breadcrumbs
2 oz (50 g) walnuts or sweet almonds, chopped
1 small egg, whisked
2 cloves garlic, crushed
½ pint (250 ml) beer
1 teaspoon (5 ml spoon) arrowroot or cornflour
salt, black pepper

If the boned joint has been rolled up undo the string and lay the piece of meat out flat.

Peel and grate the apple and put it in a mixing bowl, stirring in a little lemon juice at the same time. Stir in the sugar, breadcrumbs, walnuts, egg and seasoning in that order. Spread the garlic over the meat and then spoon the stuffing on to it or into any pockets in the meat (this will depend on how it has been boned). Roll the meat up round the stuffing and fasten with string or skewers. Smear the joint all over with oil, score the thick skin well with a sharp knife if not already done, and rub with coarse salt to make good, crisp crackling.

Heat the oven to Gas Mark 8/450°F/230°C. Put the joint in a roasting pan towards the top of the oven for 20 minutes, then move it to the centre of the oven and turn the heat down to Gas Mark 4/350°F/180°C for another 2–2½ hours, basting occasionally.

Half to three-quarters of an hour before you remove the joint, tip out the fat and pour the beer into the roasting pan. This will produce a delicious gravy which you can thicken with the arrowroot or cornflour dissolved in a little water and bubbled up with the juices in the pan when you have removed the joint.

Pocketed Pork Pâté

Serves 6–8

In this easily made and unusual pâté the meat is pocketed between two layers of a herb and cream cheese mixture.

1 lb (400 g) fresh minced pork
1 tablespoon (15 ml spoon) fat (preferably bacon or pork fat)
2 teaspoons (2 × 5 ml spoon) French mustard
1 oz (25 g) fresh brown breadcrumbs
8 oz (200 g) cream cheese, at room temperature
2 tablespoons (2 × 15 ml spoon) single cream or top of the milk
1 teaspoon (5 ml spoon) dried oregano
salt, black pepper

Melt the fat in a pan and fry the minced pork in it, turning it constantly with a wooden spoon until cooked. Then stir in the mustard, breadcrumbs and add salt and pepper to taste. Fry for a moment more and then leave to get almost cold.

Mix the cream cheese with the single cream and beat with a wooden spoon until smooth. Then stir in the oregano and salt and pepper to taste. Spread half the mixture on the bottom of a pâté dish, followed by the cooled mince and then topped with the remaining cream cheese. Smooth top and chill well in the fridge before serving with toast or French bread.

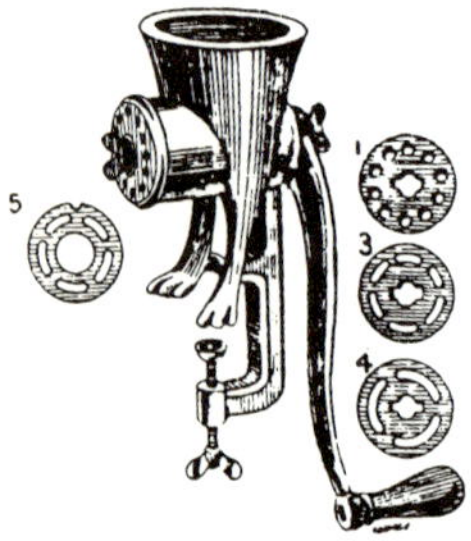

Pocketed Pork Pâté

Spinach Stuffed with Pork, Cheese and Mushrooms

Serves 6

Spinach was my favourite vegetable as a child and I still think it one of the best flavoured and most versatile. On holiday in Devon my mother-in-law's kitchen garden was bursting with spinach and it was a challenge to think up continual new ways of serving it. Luckily my children love it as much as I did at their age, but this tasty and moist way of stuffing and baking it is particularly successful. It is also another welcome way of cooking minced meat.

1 lb (400 g) fresh minced pork (or beef)
2–4 oz (50–100 g) mushrooms, chopped
2–3 cloves garlic, finely chopped
2 rounded teaspoons (2 × 5 ml spoon) paprika
4 oz (100 g) grated cheese
1 teaspoon (5 ml spoon) sugar
1 lb (400 g) spinach
a little butter or margarine
salt, black pepper

Heat the oven to Gas Mark 6/400°F/200°C.

In a bowl mix together the pork, mushrooms, garlic, paprika, 3 oz (75 g) of the grated cheese, the sugar and plenty of salt and black pepper.

Butter a fairly shallow ovenproof dish. Wash the spinach and take the stalks off. Lay about half the spinach leaves on the bottom and up the sides of the dish. Spoon in the pork mixture and cover with the remaining spinach. Sprinkle the rest of the grated cheese on top and dot with butter. Cover tightly with buttered foil or a lid and bake below the centre of the oven for $\frac{3}{4}$–1 hour. If you like, sprinkle on a little extra grated cheese before serving.

Bacon Cooked in Beer

Serves 6–8

You can use the cheapest piece of bacon you can find for this pot roast. Surrounded by an excellent vegetable sauce, it will stretch a long way and be full of flavour.

3–4 lb (1.2–1.6 kg) inexpensive bacon joint on the bone
2–3 onions, sliced
5–6 cloves
1 teaspoon (5 ml spoon) caraway seeds
8 oz (200 g) carrots, cut into chunks
1 dessertspoon (10 ml spoon) soft brown sugar
½ pint (250 ml) beer (stout for preference)
14 oz (397 g) tin tomatoes
1 level tablespoon (15 ml spoon) cornflour
black pepper

Soak the bacon in cold water for several hours – overnight if possible – changing the water once or twice.

Put the bacon into a large saucepan, cover with water, bring to the boil and simmer gently for about 15 minutes. Drain, rinse with cold water, slit the thick skin and peel it off.

Put the joint in a casserole dish with the onions, cloves, caraway seeds, carrots and sugar. Pour in the beer and the tomatoes and season with black pepper but no salt. Bring to simmering either on top of the stove or in a hot oven and then cook in the oven at Gas Mark 2/300°F/150°C for 2–3 hours, basting the bacon with the juices occasionally, until the bacon is very tender and falling from the bone.

Remove the joint to a carving board and pour the vegetables and juice into a saucepan. Dissolve the cornflour in a little water, add to the vegetables and juices, bring to the boil and bubble for 2–3 minutes. Serve with the bacon, accompanied by boiled potatoes.

Sweet and Sour Spare Ribs

Serves 6

A pile of roasted pork spare ribs coated in their shiny, rich sauce both look and taste delicious, and they are as easy as anything to prepare. Serve them with buttered noodles and a salad.

2 lb (800 g) spare ribs of pork
1 tablespoon (15 ml spoon) clear honey
2 tablespoons (2 × 15 ml spoon) marmalade
2 tablespoons (2 × 15 ml spoon) soy sauce
1 tablespoon (15 ml spoon) tomato ketchup
1 tablespoon (15 ml spoon) wine vinegar
1 rounded teaspoon (5 ml spoon) paprika
pinch of cayenne pepper
1 clove garlic, crushed
a little finely chopped spring onion or parsley for garnish
a little salt and pepper

Make sure the spare ribs are cut into single ribs and then put them in a roasting pan.

Heat the oven to Gas Mark 4/350°F/180°C.

Mix all the other ingredients together in a bowl and smear the mixture thickly all over the spare ribs. Roast in the centre of the oven for 45 minutes, basting now and then and turning the ribs over once.

Transfer the ribs to a serving dish. Bubble the pan juices over a strong heat until reduced and thickened. Spoon this thick, shiny sauce over the spare ribs and sprinkle with a little chopped spring onion or parsley. Eat with your fingers, of course!

Sweet and Sour Spare Ribs

Lamb

'Be rather bountiful than expensive.'
William Penn

Having lived in the Middle East I have a particular *penchant* for lamb, which they cook in so many delicious and different ways. In England we seem to get rather stuck on lamb chops, roast lamb with mint sauce and Irish stew. Fortunately, you can now buy minced lamb quite easily, which to my mind is better than minced beef for meatballs and much more suitable for shepherd's pie.

Lamb should always be very well seasoned. It is an excellent stewing meat, as within a very short time it becomes meltingly tender.

Lamb Cooked in Milk

Serves 4

This casserole can be made using the cheapest stewing lamb. It has a mild, delicate flavour and smooth consistency.

a little cooking fat or oil
1 teaspoon (5 ml spoon) sugar
1¼–1½ lb (500–600 g) stewing lamb
1 level tablespoon (15 ml spoon) plain flour
1 pint (500 ml) milk
1 oz (25 g) pearl barley
5–6 sticks celery, sliced
1 onion, sliced thinly in rings
a little butter or margarine
a little top of the milk
juice of half a lemon
¼–½ whole nutmeg, grated
salt, black pepper

Heat the oven to Gas Mark 9/475°F/240°C.

Melt a little fat in a large frying pan, add the sugar and fry the lamb until browned all over. Drain off the fat and transfer the meat to a casserole dish.

Blend the flour in a jug or bowl with a little of the milk until smooth. Add the rest of the milk, season with salt and black pepper and pour over the lamb. Add the pearl barley and celery. Cover and cook in the oven until simmering (15–20 minutes) and, turning the oven down to Gas Mark 2/300°F/150°C, cook for another 1¼–1½ hours.

Fry the onion in a little butter over a strong heat until golden brown. Stir some top of the milk, the lemon juice and the nutmeg into the casserole, sprinkle the fried onions on the top and serve accompanied by minty green peas and new potatoes or buttered noodles.

Minced Lamb with Creamy Cheese Topping

Serves 6–8

This is most suitable for a large family meal at weekends. It takes very little time to make, and both adults and children enjoy the mixture of the tasty lamb with its toasted cheese topping.

1 teaspoon (5 ml spoon) cooking fat or oil
1 medium-size onion, sliced and chopped roughly
1½ lb (600 g) fresh minced lamb
1–2 cloves garlic, chopped or crushed
2 teaspoons (2 × 5 ml spoon) dried thyme (or a little more fresh thyme)
1 oz (25 g) ground almonds
salt, black pepper

For the topping
1 pint (500 ml) milk
1 oz (25 g) cornflour
4 oz (100 g) grated cheese
a little butter or margarine
salt, black pepper

Heat the fat or oil in a large frying pan. Fry the onion for a minute or two and then add the lamb, garlic and thyme. Cook quickly over a strong heat, stirring the mixture constantly; then pour off any excess fat and add plenty of salt and black pepper to taste. Lastly, stir in the ground almonds. Transfer the mixture to an ovenproof dish, pat down and keep warm while you make the topping.

Put the milk in a saucepan, blend the cornflour with a little cold water and stir into the milk. Bring to the boil, stirring all the time and simmer for about 2 minutes. Stir in all but a tablespoon (15 ml spoon) of the cheese, salt and black pepper and continue stirring until the cheese has melted.

Pour the sauce over the lamb and sprinkle the remaining cheese on top. Dot with butter or margarine. Put under a medium grill until golden brown and serve with a green salad or green vegetable.

Mushroom-stuffed Lamb in Herb Pastry

Serves 4–5

In this recipe an inexpensive piece of best end of neck of lamb is transformed into an impressive dinner party dish. The smell of the herb pastry cooking is mouthwatering.

For the pastry
4 oz (100 g) butter or margarine
8 oz (200 g) strong plain flour
½ teaspoon (2.5 ml spoon) salt
1–2 teaspoons (1–2 × 5 ml spoon) fresh or dried thyme
1 teaspoon (5 ml spoon) dried oregano or marjoram
black pepper

For the filling
1 large clove garlic
1½–1¾ lbs (600–700 g) best end of neck of lamb
¼ lb (100 g) mushrooms
coarsely grated peel of 1 lemon
1 egg, lightly whisked
a spot of milk
salt, black pepper

To make the pastry, cut the fat into the flour and then crumble in your fingers until the mixture is like breadcrumbs. Using a knife, stir in the salt, herbs, a good sprinkling of black pepper and a very little cold water until the mixture only just begins to stick together. Gather up into a ball, wrap in plastic or foil and chill in the fridge for as long as possible, or at least while you prepare the meat.

Slice the garlic and put it between the chops. Cut the mushrooms up into small pieces and mix with the lemon peel, salt and black pepper. Bind together with the egg. Spoon this mixture on to the joint between the chops and the long end and press some stuffing in between each. Then bring the long end up round the stuffing and tie loosely together with string.

Heat the oven to Gas Mark 4/350°F/180°C. Roll out the pastry into a piece large enough to wrap the joint with. Moisten the edges, put the meat on the pastry, fat side down, and wrap up like a parcel, pressing the edges to seal.

Put the pastry parcel into a greased roasting pan, join side down, and cut two slits in the top for the steam to escape. (If there is time, put back into the fridge for a while before cooking, as this helps the pastry keep its shape.) Brush all over with milk and cook in the centre of the oven for 1½–1¾ hours. If the pastry gets too brown lay a piece of foil on top.

The easiest way to slice the joint is to remove the top piece of the pastry, remembering to give each person a good piece of it while serving out.

Turkish Meatballs in Egg and Lemon Sauce

Serves 3–4

I was given this recipe by a private chef in Istanbul. It is a peasant dish which he was brought up on but still makes today for his rich employers. The smooth, lemony sauce is delicious and I find it an ideal family dish.

1 lb (400 g) minced lamb (or pork or beef)
4 oz (100 g) rice
a handful of parsley, chopped finely
1 onion, chopped finely
1 egg
juice of 2 small lemons
2 level dessertspoons (2 × 10 ml spoon) plain flour
1 teaspoon (5 ml spoon) paprika
1 oz (25 g) butter
salt, black pepper

Mix the chopped onion and parsley with the minced meat. Stir in the rice, salt and plenty of black pepper. Form into small balls, each the size of a marble (this is easier to do with wet hands).

Bring $1\frac{3}{4}$ pints (875 ml) salted water to the boil in a large pan. Drop in the meatballs and when the water returns to the boil remove any scum. Simmer gently for half an hour.

In a small saucepan whisk the egg, lemon juice, 4 fl oz (100 ml) water and the flour. Bring to the boil slowly, stirring all the time. If it seems to thicken too much, add just a little more water. Then stir the mixture gradually into the meatballs and water.

Before serving, melt the butter with the paprika, cook gently for 3 minutes and trickle it over the top.

Turkish Meatballs in Egg and Lemon Sauce, in preparation

Breast of Lamb with Special Stuffing

Serves 5–6

There can hardly be a cheaper roast than a breast of lamb, yet if you take the trouble to make an unusual and aromatic stuffing it can be as good as a much more expensive piece of meat.

2 oz (50 g) pearl barley, boiled until soft
2–3 oz (50–75 g) spinach leaves, chopped finely
1 oz (25 g) shelled brazil nuts, chopped
2 cloves garlic, chopped finely
1 rounded teaspoon (5 ml spoon) fresh or dried thyme
1 large, boned, breast of lamb
1 egg, lightly whisked
salt, black pepper

Boil the pearl barley beforehand and heat the oven to Gas Mark 3/325°F/160°C.

Mix the pearl barley, spinach, nuts, garlic and thyme together thoroughly in a bowl. Season with salt and black pepper and stir in the whisked egg.

Lay the breast of lamb out flat and spoon the stuffing on it. Bring the lamb up round the stuffing and secure with one or two skewers – some of the stuffing is bound to fall out as you do this, but just press it in again afterwards as much as possible and the egg will bind it together as it cooks.

Rub the outside of the lamb with oil and a little salt. Cook in the centre of the oven for about 2 hours, basting occasionally.

Minty Lamb Stew

Serves 4–6

In England one is used to mint sauce as an accompaniment to roast lamb but in the Middle East lamb is often cooked with fresh mint and the result is quite different, tasty and refreshing. This economical stew is very easy to make and you will find it is extremely popular with all the family.

1½–2 lb (600–800 g) stewing lamb
2 large onions, sliced in rings
2–3 large cooking tomatoes, skinned and chopped
1–2 large cloves garlic, chopped (optional)
a large handful of mint, chopped
juice of 1 lemon
¾–1 pint (375–500 ml) good stock
plenty of salt and black pepper

Simply put all the ingredients into a large casserole dish. Bring to the boil on top of the stove and then simmer in the oven at Gas Mark 3/325°F/160°C for 1½–2 hours, until the meat is tender.

Serve with buttered boiled potatoes and carrots.

Shoulder of Lamb with Leek and Turnip Stuffing

Serves 6–8

The addition of an unusual stuffing can enhance the Sunday joint, or make a succulent dish for a dinner party. This mild and simple stuffing goes well with the new season's lamb. Although you could bone the joint yourself with a sharp knife, try to ask the butchery department in advance to do this for you and to leave it unrolled.

1½–2 oz (35–50 g) fresh breadcrumbs
2 small turnips, coarsely grated
2 leeks, chopped small
3–4 teaspoons (3–4 × 5 ml spoon) fresh mustard
2 teaspoons (2 × 5 ml spoon) grated nutmeg
1 egg, beaten
3½–4½ lb (1.4–1.8 kg) joint of shoulder of lamb
a little oil
salt, black pepper

Simply mix all the stuffing ingredients in a bowl, season very generously with salt and pepper and bind together with the egg. Press this mixture into any pockets in the boned lamb or make incisions with a knife if there aren't enough places to press the stuffing into. Roll together fairly loosely, trying to encase all the stuffing, and then hold together with skewers or string. Rub the joint all over with oil and salt and put in a roasting pan.

Heat the oven to Gas Mark 3/325°F/160°C. Cook the lamb in the centre of the oven, basting occasionally, for 2–2½ hours.

To make a delicious sauce for this joint, make an ordinary white sauce, season it well and stir any juices from the joint into it together with 2 teaspoons (2 × 5 ml spoon) mustard and 1 teaspoon (5 ml spoon) grated nutmeg.

Chicken and Rabbit

'I want there to be no peasant in my kingdom so poor that he is unable to have a chicken in his pot every Sunday.'

Henry IV of France

Roast chicken is a family favourite and lends itself to all manner of sauces and methods of cooking.

To me the flavour of rabbit is even more interesting than that of chicken, although some people are still prejudiced against it. But now that rabbit is plentiful again, carefully bred and still inexpensive, I feel that it is time to give it another try.

Moroccan Lemon Chicken

Serves 4

At the foot of the Atlas Mountains, in the south of Morocco, lies the beautiful walled city of Marrakech. We have spent two fascinating winter holidays there.

One of the most famous local dishes is a pigeon pie covered with the finest flaky pastry you have ever seen and sprinkled with icing sugar. You could hardly attempt this thousand-leafed pastry at home but there is another very popular and more homely dish, lemon chicken. Here is my simple adaptation of it. The traditional recipe would not include the beans (which you can omit if you like), but I think they absorb the delicious sauce very well. For this dish you can use boiling fowl, but if you can't get one reduce the cooking time by half an hour.

8 oz (200 g) dried butter beans or haricot beans
a little butter or margarine
1 onion, sliced
2–3 large cloves garlic, chopped finely
4 joints boiling fowl
a handful of fresh mint leaves, chopped finely (optional)
1 lemon, sliced in thin rounds
1 pint (500 ml) well-seasoned stock
3–4 tablespoons (3–4 × 15 ml spoon) plain yoghurt

Soak the beans for 8 hours, or overnight, in cold water. When soaked, simmer them gently in unsalted water for about half an hour. Drain, rinse and put into a large casserole.

Heat the oven to Gas Mark 9/475°F/240°C. Melting the butter in a large frying pan, fry the onion until light brown, add the garlic and fry for a minute or two longer. Stir the mixture into the beans.

Put a little more fat in the pan if necessary and fry the chicken joints all over until golden brown. Arrange them on top of the beans, sprinkle the chopped mint over and around them and arrange the lemon slices underneath and on top. Then pour over the stock, which must be extra-well seasoned. Cover and cook in the oven until simmering – about 20 minutes – then turn down to Gas Mark 1/275°F/140°C for a further 1½–2 hours, until the chicken is tender.

Before serving, spoon the yoghurt over the top.

Joints of Chicken Baked with Honey and Ginger

Serves 6

If you buy the cheaper frozen chicken joints this easy way of cooking makes them a juicy and original dish. Fresh ginger, if you can get it, is particularly delicious, but crystallised ginger will do. It is the combination of flavours, of sweet and sour, which makes the juices so good. Any joints of chicken can be used, even the inexpensive wings.

6 joints of chicken
2 tablespoons (2 × 15 ml spoon) vegetable oil
a handful of fresh mint, chopped
2 teaspoons (2 × 5 ml spoon) fresh or dried rosemary
2 cloves garlic, chopped
1–1½ inch (2–3 cm) piece of fresh root ginger or 1 tablespoon (15 ml spoon) crystallised ginger, finely chopped
1 dessertspoon (10 ml spoon) candied peel
4–6 oz (100–150 g) mushrooms, sliced
a generous sprinkling of soy sauce
1 tablespoon (15 ml spoon) honey
1 tablespoon (15 ml spoon) oil
salt, black pepper

Heat the oven to Gas Mark 4/350°F/180°C.

Fry the chicken joints in the oil until golden and place them in a large, fairly shallow, ovenproof dish. Sprinkle the mint, rosemary, garlic, ginger, peel, salt and black pepper on both sides of the chicken. Arrange the mushrooms both underneath and above the joints. Sprinkle on the soy sauce and spoon over the honey and oil. Cover the dish with foil or a lid and cook in the oven for 1¼–1½ hours.

Joints of Chicken Baked with Honey and Ginger, in preparation

Rabbit in the Orchard Pie

Serves 6

This is a rather special pie with a deliciously creamy filling and rich, melting pastry. As the sauce is so good you can use the inexpensive frozen rabbit imported from China.

For the pastry
8 oz (200 g) strong plain flour
½ teaspoon (2.5 ml spoon) salt
4 oz (100 g) butter or margarine
2 oz (50 g) lard

For the filling
1 oz (25 g) butter or margarine
1¼–1½ lb (500–600 g) boneless (or 2½ lb, 1 kg, whole) rabbit
1 tablespoon (15 ml spoon) plain flour
½ pint (250 ml) cider or milk
3 teaspoons (3 × 15 ml spoon) fresh or 2 teaspoons (2 × 5 ml spoon) dried tarragon
1 teaspoon (5 ml spoon) French mustard
5 fl oz (125 ml) soured cream
1 apple, peeled, cored and thinly sliced
2 oz (50 g) mushrooms, sliced
salt, black pepper

Make the pastry first. Sift the flour and salt into a bowl, cut in the fat and crumble with your fingertips until the mixture looks like rough breadcrumbs. Add a very little, very cold, water (the less you add the more crumbly the pastry will be) and stir in with a knife until the pastry just begins to stick together. Gather up and form into a ball, wrap in plastic or foil and put in the fridge.

Heat the oven to Gas Mark 4/350°F/180°C. Melt the butter in a large frying pan and remove from the heat. Stir the rabbit in the butter and mix in the flour. Add the cider, put the pan back over the heat and stir until it bubbles and thickens. Then put in the tarragon, mustard, salt and black pepper. Transfer the mixture to a casserole, cover and cook in the oven for 1 hour.

Remove from the oven, stir in the soured cream, sliced apple and mushrooms and transfer the mixture to a suitably sized pie dish or earthenware flan dish. Allow to cool.

When the filling is cold, heat the oven to Gas Mark 6/400°F/200°C, knead the pastry slightly, and roll out fairly thickly into a piece big enough to cover the pie dish. Moisten the edges of the dish and lay the pastry on top. Press the edges down lightly on to the rim and trim neatly. Roll out the trimmings to decorate. Brush with a little milk, or, for a beautifully golden glaze, a little egg yolk, and cook in the centre of the oven for 25–30 minutes.

Chicken and Fish Casserole with Lemon

Serves 4

You wouldn't imagine it, but the flavours of chicken and smoked fish are delicious together, making this simple dish into something quite special.

4 smallish joints of chicken, with the skin removed
4 pieces smoked cod, haddock or whiting, about 10 oz (250g) weight
½ lb (100 g) cooking tomatoes, chopped
1 green or red pepper, chopped
1 large lemon, sliced in rounds
1–2 cloves garlic, chopped (optional)
approx. 8 fl oz (200 ml) chicken stock
2 teaspoons (2 × 5 ml spoon) fresh or dried tarragon
salt, black pepper

Heat the oven to Gas Mark 6/400°F/200°C.

Put the chicken joints into a casserole dish. Add the tomatoes, pepper, lemon and garlic, with salt and pepper, to the chicken. Pour over the chicken stock. Put the lid on the dish and cook for 20 minutes.

Add the fish and tarragon and continue cooking for another 25–30 minutes.

Serve with rice.

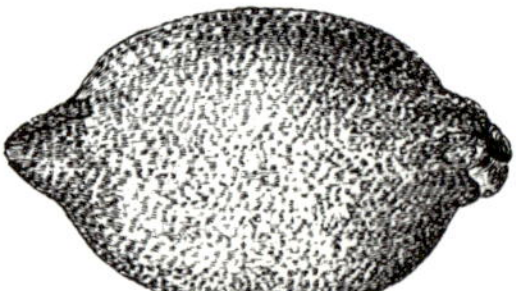

Chicken and Fish Casserole with Lemon

Rabbit in Parsnip and Mushroom Sauce

Serves 4

Frozen rabbit joints are inexpensive and taste excellent if casseroled in a good sauce. This one has a subtle and rather nutty flavour.

2 oz (50 g) butter or margarine
4 joints of rabbit, approx. $1\frac{1}{4}$–$1\frac{1}{2}$ lb (500–600 g) weight
8 oz (200 g) parsnips, peeled and grated coarsely
2 teaspoons (2×5 ml spoon) plain flour
1 pint (500 ml) warm milk (or milk and stock)
1–2 teaspoons ($1–2 \times 5$ ml spoon) French mustard
$\frac{1}{4}$ lb (100 g) mushrooms, sliced thinly
$\frac{1}{4}$ whole nutmeg, grated
a little plain yoghurt or single cream

Heat oven to Gas Mark 3/325°F/160°C.

Melt the butter in a large, heavy saucepan or iron casserole. Stir the rabbit and parsnips into the fat and then stir in the flour. Add the warm milk, mustard, salt and black pepper. Bring to the boil, stirring, and simmer for 2–3 minutes.

Then, if using a saucepan, transfer to a casserole, cover and simmer in the oven for $1\frac{1}{2}$–2 hours or until the rabbit is tender.

Five or ten minutes before serving add the mushrooms and nutmeg to the casserole and return to the oven. Just before serving, roughly stir in the yoghurt or cream.

Offal

'Economy is of itself a great revenue.'
Cicero

How often do mothers say to their child, as he sits dejectedly in front of his plate of dry, overcooked liver, 'Eat it up, it's so good for you' – thereupon probably putting him off liver for life. At his school even worse cooking will probably reinforce his hatred of all offal.

Unfortunately it is true that offal, with its unappetising name, has gained a bad reputation through careless cooking and through a general feeling that, although undeniably 'good' for you, it is very definitely second-rate food. What we forget is that, quite apart from being highly nutritious and far cheaper than the main cuts of meat, it can have a much better flavour. So the secret is to get the texture right by cooking the offal in the proper way.

In the following recipes I have tried to give examples of how either very quick cooking or long, slow cooking, depending on the type of offal, can give delicious results.

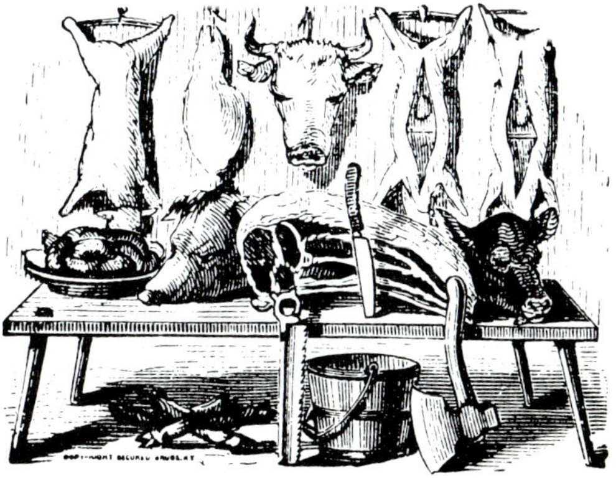

Apple-topped Kidneys with Rice

Serves 4–5

Pig's kidneys are both inexpensive and full of flavour. This satisfying dish of tender braised kidneys in a rich, fruity sauce with a crunchy rice and apple top seems to please even the professed kidney-haters!

1 lb (400 g) pig's kidneys
1 oz (25 g) cooking fat
1 large onion, sliced
1 rounded tablespoon (15 ml spoon) plain flour
½ pint (125 ml) sweet cider
½ teaspoon (2.5 ml spoon) plus ¼ teaspoon (½ × 2.5 ml spoon) ground cinnamon
3–4 cooking tomatoes, sliced
1 oz (25 g) currants
1 large cup (200 g) rice
2½ large cups (500 ml) salted, boiling water
1 egg, lightly whisked
1 large eating apple
butter
salt, black pepper

Heat the oven to Gas Mark 9/475°F/240°C.

Skin the kidneys and cut into thin slices. Melt the fat in a large frying pan. Brown the onion over a strong heat, add the kidneys and cook quickly to seal. Remove from the heat and stir in the flour. Then add the cider and return to the heat. Simmer for 2–3 minutes, stirring, until the sauce is fairly thick. Season with salt, black pepper and the larger portion of ground cinnamon. Add the tomatoes and currants.

Transfer the mixture to a fairly shallow ovenproof dish. Cover with a piece of foil and cook in the centre of the oven for about 20 minutes until simmering. Then turn down the oven to Gas Mark 3/325°F/160°C and continue cooking for 1–1½ hours.

Before the mixture has quite finished cooking, boil the rice in the water until just tender – it should still have a slight bite to it. After draining in a sieve and rinsing with hot water mix the rice in a bowl with the whisked egg and season with black pepper and a little salt.

Heat the grill. Spoon the rice on top of the kidneys. Slice the apple thinly and arrange neatly on top of the rice. Sprinkle over the remaining cinnamon and dot all over with butter. Grill until the apples are browned.

Tripe in Oregano Sauce

Serves 4–6

I have eaten tripe in restaurants abroad and always disliked it, but a book of economical food would obviously not be complete without a recipe for tripe. So, grudgingly, I bought an unappetising, rubbery white mass of tripe to try, feeling that the only pleasure in the resulting dish would be its low price and high nutritional content. However, I was in for a surprise. Melt-in-the-mouth tripe cooked in this smooth, flavourful sauce of onions and tomatoes with a cheesy top is quite delicious. Even the children liked it, because they didn't have to chew!

1 lb (400 g) ox tripe
3 large onions, roughly chopped
¾ pint (375 ml) milk
2 cooking tomatoes
2 oz (50 g) butter or margarine
2 oz (50 g) plain flour
1 rounded teaspoon (5 ml spoon) dried oregano
2 oz (50 g) grated cheese
salt, black pepper

Cut the tripe into 1 inch (2 cm) pieces and put into a heavy-based saucepan with the chopped onions. Pour in the milk, cover the pan and bring to the boil. Then simmer gently for ¾–1 hour or until the tripe is tender but still has a very slight bite to it. Strain off the liquid into a bowl and leave on one side.

Put the tripe and onions into a shallow ovenproof dish. Cut each tomato in six and arrange in the dish with the tripe. Melt the butter in a pan and stir in the flour. Gradually stir in the strained-off liquid. Bring to the boil, stirring all the time, and then simmer, still stirring, for 2–3 minutes. Season to taste with salt and black pepper and add the oregano. Pour this sauce over the tripe and sprinkle the grated cheese on top.

Heat the oven to Gas Mark 5/375°F/190°C and cook towards the top for 30–40 minutes until golden brown.

For a light meal you could serve it just with a green salad, but for hungry people it is very good with carrots and boiled potatoes.

Parsley-stuffed Tongue

Will serve 15 or more guests

If you are having a party or have a lot of people to feed during the summer a pressed ox tongue will go a long way. People are put off by its appearance when uncooked and think that the preparation must be arduous. If fact, it is very simple and the tender texture and mild flavour are excellent.

1 pickled ox tongue
1 onion, sliced roughly
2 bay leaves
6–7 cloves
8–10 peppercorns
a handful of fresh parsley, chopped finely

Soak the tongue in cold water for at least 2 hours and then put it in a saucepan with the onion, bay leaves, cloves and peppercorns. Add water to cover, bring to the boil and simmer steadily for 3–3½ hours. Plunge the tongue into a sink of cold water and remove the little bones and the skin.

Lightly oil a round cake tin or dish, just large enough to take the tongue. Curl the tongue round and press the parsley down into the slight gaps. Pour in just enough of the cooking liquid to cover the tongue. Put a small plate which just fits inside the tin on top of the tongue and weight it down as heavily as possible. Leave to cool and then refrigerate until next day.

When ready to serve, remove the plate and carefully loosen the sides with a knife. Plop the tongue out on to a serving plate.

Parsley-stuffed Tongue

Creamy Kidneys

Serves 4

Pig's kidneys are still inexpensive and this way of cooking them makes a delicious sauce, tasty but mild, which is excellent with rice.

4 pig's kidneys, about 1 lb (400 g) weight
2 oz (50 g) fat
1–2 cloves garlic, chopped finely
1 heaped tablespoon (2 × 15 ml spoon) plain flour
a pinch of cayenne pepper
½ pint (250 ml) hot milk
2–3 oz (50–75 g) mushrooms, sliced thinly
4 tablespoons (4 × 15 ml spoon) plain yoghurt
a little finely chopped fresh mint or parsley for garnish

Soak the kidneys for at least 1 hour in cold water. Then cut away the white cores and slice thinly.

Melt the fat in a heavy-based saucepan and add the chopped garlic, followed by the kidneys. Stir and cook over a strong heat for a moment or two. Remove from the heat, stir in the flour and cayenne pepper and add the hot milk. Bring to the boil, stirring, and then cover the pan and simmer very gently for ¾–1 hour, stirring occasionally.

Stir in the mushrooms and the yoghurt. Leave over the heat for 2–3 minutes but don't boil. Pour into a serving dish and sprinkle with the mint or parsley.

Poor Man's Goose

Serves 4

This is a homely recipe which came from an old cookery book belonging to my grandmother and I was attracted to it by its title, apart from the obvious economy of a satisfying dish made from pig's liver. The smooth texture and flavour is, in fact, slightly similar to that of goose – but without all the fat, of course.

1 lb (400 g) pig's liver
1 rounded tablespoon (2 × 10 ml spoon) well-seasoned plain flour
1 onion, chopped finely
a handful of fresh sage leaves, chopped finely, or 2 teaspoons (2 × 5 ml spoon) dried sage
1–1½ lb (400–600 g) potatoes, parboiled and sliced
¼ pint (125 ml) hot water
a little butter or margarine
salt, black pepper

Heat oven to Gas Mark 4/350°F/180°C.

Slice the liver thinly and dip into the flour. Put in the bottom of an ovenproof dish. Mix the onion and sage together, sprinkle with salt and pepper and add to the liver. Arrange the sliced potatoes on top. Pour the water over, sprinkle the potatoes with salt and pepper and dot them with butter. Cook, uncovered, in the centre of the oven for about 1½ hours.

Sweetbreads in Creamy Mustard Sauce

Serves 4

Sweetbreads are mild and tender and the combination of textures and flavours makes this a delicate and unusual dish, which should even convert some offal haters.

¾ lb (300 g) sweetbreads
1 lb (400 g) parsnips
seasoned flour
good dripping or bacon fat
¼ lb (100 g) mushrooms
1 oz (25 g) butter or margarine
½ oz (15 g) cornflour
a little over ½ pint (250 ml) milk
1 teaspoon (5 ml spoon) white wine vinegar
1 teaspoon (5 ml spoon) mild French mustard
1 tablespoon (15 ml spoon) plain yoghurt or single cream
salt, black pepper

Soak the sweetbreads in salted water for 2–3 hours, changing the water occasionally to drain away any blood. Peel the parsnips, slice into rather thin rounds and boil in salted water until tender. Drain.

Bring the sweetbreads to the boil in a pan of salted water, drain at once and rinse them under cold water. Cut into small pieces, removing any black veins – recipes always tell you to remove these black veins but no sweetbreads I buy ever seem to have any! Dip in seasoned flour. Melt about a tablespoon (15 ml spoon) of fat in a pan and fry the sweetbreads until golden brown all over. Transfer to a serving dish and keep warm.

Put some more fat into the pan and fry the parsnip slices until brown on both sides. Mix them with the sweetbreads. Slice the mushrooms thinly, add some more fat and just toss the mushrooms around over the heat for not more than a minute – they should not become soft. Mix them in with the sweetbreads and parsnips and continue to keep warm.

Melt the butter in a saucepan and stir in the cornflour until smooth. Add the milk, bring to the boil and bubble for 2–3 minutes, stirring all the time. Then add the vinegar and mustard and season to taste with salt and black pepper. Stir in the yoghurt or cream, pour the resulting sauce over the sweetbread mixture and serve accompanied by broad beans or peas, and sauté potatoes.

Sweetbreads in Creamy Mustard Sauce

Warm-hearted Casserole

Serves 4

A comforting dish for cold winter days. Ox heart cooked as long and slowly as possible makes a lovely rich sauce and the addition of the streaky belly of pork gives it that extra bit of flavour.

¾ lb (300 g) ox heart
just over 1 oz (25 g) cooking fat
2 rounded tablespoons (2 × 15 ml spoon) plain flour
2 medium-sized onions, sliced
2–3 cooking tomatoes, sliced roughly
2 carrots, sliced
¾ pint (375 ml) well-seasoned beef stock
1 rounded teaspoon (5 ml spoon) paprika
½ lb (200 g) belly of pork, with the rind cut off

Cut away any gristle and tubes from the heart and cut into small, thin slices.

Melt 1 oz (25 g) of fat in a pan and fry the pieces of heart until just brown. Remove from the heat and stir in the flour. Transfer to a casserole dish.

Melt a little more fat in the pan and fry the onions until brown. Add them to the casserole. Then add the tomatoes and carrots, pour over the stock and stir in the paprika.

Heat the oven to Gas Mark 8–9/450–475°F/230–240°C. Cover the casserole and cook in the oven for 20–25 minutes or until bubbling. Then turn down to Gas Mark 1/275°F/140°C and cook further for about 2 hours.

Slice the pork into smallish pieces and add to the casserole. Continue cooking at Gas Mark ½–1/250–275°F/120–140°C for 2–3 hours – the longer the better, really.

Serve with boiled carrots and potatoes.

Fish

'Thou shall have a fishy on a little dishy,
Thou shall have a fishy when the boat comes in.'
Nineteenth-century Folk Song

Fish is another food, like offal, which many people have been turned against by having it so often badly cooked during their childhood. Like offal, it is extremely nutritious and by no means difficult to cook if you know how to treat it.

Although it is more expensive nowadays than of old, fish takes only a short time to cook, so that you will save on your gas or electricity. Since its character and the kind of dishes you can make with it are so completely different from that of meat, to have fish at least once a week gives a refreshing variation to your diet.

Curried Fish and Onion Puff

Serves 4

An easily made and unusual lunch or supper dish. I like it with a bowl of plain yoghurt to spoon over as a sauce, accompanied by a good mixed salad.

2 medium-sized onions
1 oz (25 g) butter or margarine
2–3 teaspoons (2–3 × 5 ml spoon) curry powder
10–12 oz (250–300 g) smoked whiting, cod or haddock fillets
1 oz (25 g) sultanas
8 oz (200 g) packet of puff pastry
a little milk or egg yolk to glaze
salt, black pepper

Slice the onions thinly and fry gently in the butter until just soft. Stir in the curry powder, remove from the heat and transfer to a bowl to cool.

If the fish is frozen, let it thaw slightly to enable you to cut it into small cubes. Mix the cut fish and the sultanas with the onions and season with just a little salt and pepper.

Heat the oven to Gas Mark 7/425°F/220°C. Cut the pastry in half and form into two balls. Roll out and shape into two 8 inch (20 cm) circles. Lay one circle on the bottom of a greased ovenproof serving dish. Spoon the cold onion and fish mixture on the pastry, leaving about 1 inch (2 cm) round the edge. Moisten this edge and lay the other circle on top, pressing the edges to seal. Pierce two holes in the top for the steam to escape. Trim the edges of the pastry and, if you like, roll out the trimmings to make pastry patterns to decorate the puff. Brush with milk or, for a beautiful gloss, a little egg yolk and cook in the centre of the oven for 25–35 minutes until the pastry is a rich golden brown.

Curried Fish and Onion Puff

Smoked Cod Fillets in Cheese and Semolina Sauce

Serves 4

I have always loved fish coated in a good cheese sauce and this dish of smoky fish, eggs and mushrooms in a more unusual sauce is always a success.

6–7 oz (150–175 g) smoked cod fillets
½ oz (15 g) semolina
¾ pint (375 ml) milk
2 large hard-boiled eggs, sliced
2 oz (50 g) mushrooms, sliced finely
1 level dessertspoon (10 ml spoon) cornflour
2 teaspoons (2 × 5 ml spoon) chopped fresh or dried chives
a little grated parmesan (or other cheese)
a little butter or margarine
salt, black pepper

Heat oven to Gas Mark 6/400°F/200°C. Put the fish in a fairly shallow ovenproof dish, dot with butter, cover and cook for 20 minutes (or 30 minutes if still frozen).

While this is cooking, put the semolina and milk in a pan, bring to the boil and then simmer gently for 20 minutes, stirring fairly often.

When the fish has cooked, pour the juices into the milk and semolina mixture, break the fish up and arrange with the hard-boiled eggs and mushrooms in the ovenproof dish.

After the semolina and milk have been simmering for 20 minutes, blend the cornflour in a spoonful of milk and add to the pan. Let the mixture bubble for a further 2–3 minutes, stirring all the time and then add the chives and salt and black pepper to taste. Pour the mixture over the fish, sprinkle generously with grated parmesan and dot with butter. Put under a hot grill until well browned and serve accompanied by a salad.

Fish and Mushroom Timbale

Serves 6–8

This unusual and delicious dish, popular with both adults and children, is an impressive and inexpensive way of feeding a crowd of hungry people. It is a straightforward recipe, but as it is cooked in stages start well in advance. If you don't like fish you can use cooked chicken instead. What I particularly like is a mixture of both. Any fish of your choice will do – smoked cod is excellent, and for a special occasion the addition of prawns, mussels or salmon will turn it into a real treat.

For the rice
1 large cup (200 g) easy-cook rice
2 oz (50 g) butter or margarine
1 onion, finely sliced
2 rounded teaspoons (2 × 5 ml spoon) curry powder

For the fish mixture
1 oz (25 g) butter or margarine
1 onion, finely sliced
¼ lb (100 g) mushrooms, sliced
8 oz (200 g) fish (see above), pre-cooked and flaked
salt, black pepper

For the crust
8 oz (200 g) packet of puff pastry
a little melted butter

First soak the rice in hot water for 20–30 minutes. Then melt the 2 oz (50 g) butter in a heavy-based saucepan and cook the onion gently in the butter until soft, but not brown. Stir in the curry powder and add a cup (the same one used to measure the rice) of water. Pour the soaked rice into a sieve, rinse well under running water and add to the saucepan. Cover, bring to the boil and simmer gently for 10–15 minutes, until the water is absorbed. Add salt to taste and leave to cool.

Meanwhile, make up the fish mixture, as follows. Melt the 1 oz (25 g) butter in a frying pan and fry the onion until it is transparent. Add the mushrooms (and a little more butter if necessary) and toss over the heat for just a minute or so. Mix in a bowl with the pre-cooked fish, season to taste with salt and black pepper and leave to cool.

When the mixture is almost cold butter a pudding basin or ovenproof bowl big enough to hold the rice and fish. Cut off three-quarters of the pastry, roll out very thinly, shaping it into a circle large enough to line the basin and to overlap the edges, so that there will be enough to fold back over the top of the filling.

Heat the oven to Gas Mark 5/375°F/190°C. Line the basin with the pastry and brush with some melted butter. Then roll out the last quarter of the pastry into a thin piece big enough to line the basin but not this time to overlap the edges; lay this piece over the other pastry. Then spoon in the rice and the fish mixture alternately in layers, starting and ending with a layer of rice. Fold the pastry edges over the filling to cover it, brushing with melted butter where the pastry overlaps.

Cook in the centre of the oven for 45 minutes, turn it out on to an ovenproof serving plate and then return it to the oven for 10–15 minutes, until the dome of pastry is golden brown all over.

Serve with a simple salad.

Fish and Mushroom Timbale

Tasty Fish Balls in Tomato Sauce

Serves 4

These tender fish balls are casseroled in a rich tomato sauce and can be made from the cheapest white fish – I use fillets of coley. As an alternative, if you have any left-over cooked fish you can use the mixture in this recipe to make fish cakes and fry them. In this case you wouldn't need the sauce.

8 oz (200 g) skinned, boned fillets of coley (if frozen, thaw first)
1 small onion, grated
3 oz (75 g) fresh white breadcrumbs
3–4 teaspoons (3–4 × 5 ml spoon) fresh or dried chopped chives or parsley
2 oz (50 g) finely grated cheese
2 teaspoons (2 × 5 ml spoon) paprika
1 egg, beaten
14 oz (397 g) tin tomatoes
2 cloves garlic, finely chopped
natural yoghurt for topping (optional)
salt, black pepper

Cut up the fish fillets roughly. Put into a liquidiser (or through a mincer) and purée. Put into a mixing bowl with the grated onion, breadcrumbs, chives, grated cheese, paprika, salt and black pepper. Bind with the egg and mix together thoroughly. Then, using damp hands, form the mixture into walnut-sized balls and fry in a little oil until a rich golden brown all over. Arrange in a shallow ovenproof dish.

Heat the oven to Gas Mark 9/475°F/240°C. Empty the tomatoes into a bowl and break up roughly with a fork. Add the garlic, salt and black pepper. Pour this sauce over the fish balls. Cover the dish with a lid or foil and cook in the oven for about 15 minutes, until bubbling, and then turn down to Gas Mark 4/350°F/180°C for another half-hour.

I think that 2–3 spoonfuls of plain yoghurt on top before you serve the dish is a good addition. Serve with rice and a green salad.

Simple Fish Stew

Serves 4

Simple to make certainly, but delicious too. This stew is very gently cooked to keep the fish moist and melting. Serve it with a bowl of easy-cook rice which has been cooked just enough to retain a slight nutty bite.

1 lb (400 g) cod (or other white fish) fillets, thawed slightly if frozen
2–3 cloves garlic, sliced finely
3 bay leaves
3–4 tomatoes, sliced
1 small red or green pepper, seeds removed and sliced thinly in rings
4 tablespoons (4 × 15 ml spoon) olive or sunflower oil
3 tablespoons (3 × 15 ml spoon) water
1 lemon
salt, black pepper

Heat oven to Gas Mark 2/300°F/150°C.

Cut the fish into 2–3 inch (5–7 cm) pieces. Using a sharp knife, make an incision in each piece of fish and insert slices of garlic and a broken piece of bay leaf. Arrange the fish in a wide, rather shallow, casserole dish and sprinkle with salt and pepper. Arrange the sliced tomatoes and peppers on top of the fish and season well again with salt and pepper. Then pour the oil and water over the mixture, cover the dish and cook in the centre of the oven for 50–60 minutes, until the fish is cooked.

To serve, cut the lemon in wedges and arrange round the edge of the uncovered dish. New potatoes, when in season, go well with this dish, but I think carefully cooked rice is best, moistened with plenty of butter or margarine.

Simple Fish Stew, in preparation

Smoky Kipper Pie

Serves 6

Almost everyone loves a fish pie, and this one has a smoky, cheesy, rich taste which makes a refreshing change from the more bland flavour of white fish.

1 lb (400 g) kipper fillets
2 oz (50 g) butter or margarine
3 oz (75 g) plain flour
1 pint (500 ml) warm milk
4 oz (100 g) grated cheese
2 teaspoons (2 × 5 ml spoon) French mustard
1 teaspoon (5 ml spoon) grated nutmeg
3 large tomatoes, peeled
1½ lb (600 g) boiled potatoes, mashed and well-buttered
salt, black pepper

If frozen, thaw the kipper fillets slightly and peel off the skins. Cut the flesh into chunks.

Melt the butter in a large saucepan. Remove from the heat and stir in the flour. Return to the heat and simmer for 2–3 minutes, stirring continuously. Gradually stir in the warm milk. When smoothly blended bring to the boil again for 2 minutes, still stirring. Reserve a spoonful of the cheese and stir the rest into the mixture with the mustard, nutmeg, salt and black pepper. Add the kipper fillets and transfer to an ovenproof dish, large enough to take the topping as well.

Slice the peeled tomatoes in rounds and arrange on top of the kipper mixture. Then spread the mashed potato on top of the tomatoes. Sprinkle over the reserved cheese, dot with butter and cook near the top of the oven at Gas Mark 4/350°F/180°C for 45 minutes, or until golden brown. Serve with a green vegetable or a salad.

Sunset Pie

Serves 6

So called because of its layers of yellow and orange ingredients, though of course to be completely realistic it should have red as well! However, it tastes lovely and makes a little fish go a long way.

10 oz (250 g) plain flour
½ teaspoon (2.5 ml spoon) salt
4 oz (100 g) butter or margarine
3 oz (75 g) lard
1 large egg (size 2), beaten
1½ lb (600 g) carrots, cooked and chopped into small pieces
2–3 smoked cod, haddock or whiting fillets, about ¾ lb (300 g) weight, cut into chunks
4 oz (100 g) grated cheese
a few coriander seeds

Make the pastry first, as follows. Sift the flour and salt into a bowl and cut in the butter and lard. Crumble the mixture with your fingertips until it looks like rough breadcrumbs. Using a knife, mix in the beaten egg until the mixture just begins to stick together. Then press into a ball with your hands, wrap in foil or plastic and chill in the fridge for at least half an hour.

Butter a 2 pint (1 litre) pie dish, cut off three-quarters of the pastry and knead it a little to make it manageable. Roll it out and line the pie dish.

Now put in the filling in layers – carrots first, then pieces of fish, then grated cheese, and so on, dotting with a few coriander seeds and seasoning with salt and pepper between each layer. End with a layer of cheese.

Knead and roll out the remaining pastry into a piece big enough for the top. Moisten the edges and lay this piece over the closely filled pie, pressing down the edges a little to seal. Make three or four holes in the top with a skewer. Trim the edges and roll out the trimmings to decorate – I always cut out a fish to swim across the top of the pie!

Heat oven to Gas Mark 4/350°F/180°C. Brush the top with a little milk and cook the pie in the centre of the oven for 1–1¼ hours.

Serve with wedges of lemon and a green salad.

Sunset Pie

Stuffed Fillets of Plaice

Serves 4

Fish and rice go well together and this way of stuffing tender fillets of plaice with a nutty pilaf rice mixture under a light, creamy sauce makes a substantial dish.

½ oz (25 g) butter or margarine
1 small onion, chopped finely
1 teaspoon (5 ml spoon) fresh or dried thyme
4 oz (100 g) easy-cook rice
4 tablespoons (4 × 15 ml spoon) water
½ egg, lightly beaten
4 plaice fillets (if frozen, allow to thaw first)
¼ pint (125 ml) single cream
1 teaspoon (5 ml) lemon juice
salt, black pepper

Melt the butter in a heavy-based saucepan and gently cook the onion in it until just softened. Add the thyme and a good sprinkling of salt and black pepper. Stir in the rice and the water. Bring to the boil, cover and simmer gently for 10–15 minutes, until the rice is cooked but still has a slight bite to it. Allow to cool and then bind the rice together with the egg.

Heat the oven to Gas Mark 6/400°F/200°C. Butter an ovenproof dish and lay out the plaice fillets in it one by one, spooning a mound of rice on to each one and then rolling the fish loosely up round the rice – it doesn't matter if it bursts out each side. Arrange the stuffed fillets closely together in a dish, dot with a little butter and sprinkle with salt and pepper. Cover with foil or a lid and cook in the oven for 25–30 minutes.

Warm the cream gently and gradually stir in the lemon juice, which will thicken it. Do not overheat the cream or it will curdle. Season to taste with salt and pepper, pour the sauce over the stuffed fillets and serve, garnished with a little chopped parsley if you wish. This dish needs only a salad as an accompaniment.

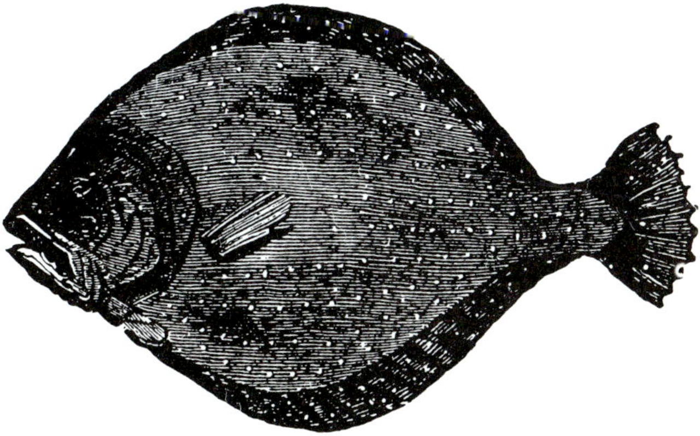

Fish Baked in Cabbage Leaves

Serves 6

This unusual way of cooking fish in tasty, tender cabbage leaves makes it especially succulent and the slices of sharp apple add a titillating tang.

1 lb (400 g) cod, whiting or haddock fillets
1 fairly large but loosely packed green cabbage, 1–1¼ lb (400–500 g) weight
1 teaspoon (5 ml spoon) paprika
1 large cooking apple, about 8 oz (200 g) weight, peeled and sliced thinly
1–2 oz (25–50 g) butter or margarine
salt, black pepper

If the fish is frozen thaw it slightly and remove the skin. Take the whole leaves off the cabbage and submerge them – you may have to do this in two or three batches – in a large pan of boiling salted water for 2 minutes. Drain and rinse with cold water.

Butter a large, but not too deep, ovenproof dish. Heat the oven to Gas Mark 5/375°F/190°C. Lay about half of the cabbage leaves on the bottom, letting them come up and overlap the sides of the dish. Lay the fish fillets on top of the cabbage leaves. Sprinkle with the paprika and with salt and pepper. Arrange the apple slices on top of the fish and dot with butter. Fold the cabbage leaves over the fish and apples and cover with the remaining leaves, pushing the cabbage in round the edges so that the fish is completely encased. Dot with some more butter, cover with foil or a lid and cook in the centre of the oven for 1 hour.

Serve with boiled potatoes.

Fish Baked in Cabbage Leaves, in preparation

Layered Fish Pie

Serves 4

I make no apology for including another fish pie recipe, as I find that variations on this theme are always welcome. The dish is a meal in itself and needs no accompanying vegetables except a simple green salad.

1 lb (400 g) frozen skinless, boneless coley
4 oz (100 g) smoked streaky bacon, with the rind cut off
1 oz (25 g) butter or margarine
1 heaped tablespoon (2 × 15 ml spoon) cornflour
½ pint (250 ml) milk
4 oz (100 g) grated cheese
a handful of parsley, chopped finely
¾ lb (300 g) carrots, boiled and sliced in rounds
1 lb (400 g) potatoes, boiled and sliced in rounds
salt, black pepper

Thaw the fish slightly. Cut into chunks and arrange in a large, shallow, greased ovenproof dish. Cut the bacon into smallish pieces and arrange amongst the fish. Cover the dish with foil and cook in the centre of the oven at Gas Mark 6/400°F/200°C for 30–35 minutes.

Meanwhile, make a cheese sauce by melting the butter in a fairly large, heavy saucepan. Take off the heat and stir in the cornflour, milk and 4 tablespoons (4 × 15 ml spoon) of water. Bring to the boil, stirring frequently, and simmer for about 3 minutes until the sauce is thick and smooth. Stir in the cheese until it melts. Turn off the heat and add the chopped parsley, salt and plenty of black pepper.

Pour the sauce over the cooked fish and arrange the carrots on top, followed by the potatoes. Dot all over with butter. If the dish is cold, reheat for about half an hour in the oven at Gas Mark 3/325°F/160°C.

Before serving, put the pie under a medium grill until the potatoes are golden brown.

Haddock and Spinach Soufflé

Serves 4

This is a complete supper dish. Apart perhaps from a slice of fresh brown bread, you need have nothing else and you should feel very satisfied!

1 oz (25 g) butter
1 level tablespoon (15 ml spoon) cornflour
½ pint (250 ml) milk
3 large eggs (size 3), separated
4–5 tablespoons (4–5 × 15 ml spoon) spinach purée
4–5 oz (100–125 g) smoked haddock, flaked
salt, black pepper

Butter a 2½ pint (1.25 litre) soufflé dish and heat the oven to Gas Mark 5/375°F/190°C.

Melt the butter in a pan and stir in the cornflour until smooth. Add the milk, bring to the boil and then simmer, stirring constantly for 2–3 minutes until smooth and thick. Transfer to a mixing bowl and stir in the egg yolks thoroughly. Add the spinach, fish and salt and pepper to taste. Whisk the egg whites until stiff and, using a metal spoon, fold lightly into the mixture.

Pour the mixture into the soufflé dish and cook in the centre of the oven for 30–40 minutes, until risen and brown on top. Serve immediately – if there has to be any delay, turn off the oven heat but don't open the oven door.

Smoked Cod Fillets in Orange and Caper Sauce

Serves 6

This easily made dish is sophisticated enough for any dinner party. The flavours combine in an unusual and mouth-watering way and the sauce is a lovely rich yellow colour.

1 lb (400 g) smoked cod
1 oz (25 g) butter or margarine
4 hard-boiled eggs, sliced
1 oz (25 g) cornflour
¾ pint (375 ml) milk
finely grated rind and juice of 1 orange
2 rounded teaspoons (2 × 5 ml spoon) capers, roughly chopped
5 fl oz (125 ml) soured cream
a little chopped parsley to garnish (optional)
salt, black pepper

Thaw the fish slightly if frozen, remove the skin and cut into largish chunks.

Heat the oven to Gas Mark 6/400°F/200°C. Lightly butter a fairly large, shallow ovenproof dish. Lay the pieces of fish in it and dot with a little butter or margarine. Cover the dish and cook just above the centre of the oven for 25–30 minutes.

Pour off the juices into a bowl and arrange the eggs in the dish on top of the fish. Cover and keep warm in the lowest oven.

Melt the 1 oz (25 g) butter in a pan, remove from the heat and stir in the cornflour until smooth. Then stir in the milk, a little at a time, and the reserved juices from the fish. Bring to the boil, stirring a little, and simmer for 2–3 minutes, stirring all the time. Add the orange rind and juice, capers, salt and black pepper. Finally, stir in the soured cream, make sure the sauce is hot, and pour it all over the fish and eggs.

Before serving sprinkle a little chopped parsley on top. New potatoes and carrots go particularly well with the sauce.

Smoked Cod Fillets in Orange and Caper Sauce

Hake Flake

Serves 6

Here is a rather different kind of fish pie which has a rich tomato sauce and a diamond-patterned flaky pastry top. My children love it. If you really object to garlic you can omit it but I feel it adds greatly to the flavour (and just think how good it is for you!).

4 frozen, skinless and boneless hake portions (or other white fish) weighing altogether 12–13 oz (300–325 g)
a little butter or margarine
14 oz (397 g) tin tomatoes
1 level tablespoon (15 ml spoon) cornflour
1 tablespoon (15 ml spoon) water
1–2 cloves garlic, crushed or chopped finely
1 rounded teaspoon (5 ml spoon) fresh or dried tarragon
8 oz (200 g) packet puff pastry
a little over 1 oz (25 g) melted butter or margarine
½–1 teaspoon (2.5–5 ml spoon) cayenne or chilli powder (optional)
salt, black pepper

Fry the fish in the butter for 5–6 minutes on each side. Transfer the pieces to a rectangular ovenproof dish, about 10 × 8 inch (25 × 20 cm), and break the fish up evenly over the bottom.

Put any remaining butter and juice with the tomatoes in a pan. Blend in a cup the cornflour with the water until smooth. Stir into the tomatoes and bring to the boil, continue stirring to break up the tomatoes and cook gently for 2–3 minutes. Remove from the heat and stir in the garlic, tarragon and salt and black pepper to taste – if you want a more piquant sauce add the cayenne or chilli powder. Pour the sauce over the fish and let cool.

Roll the pastry out to the size of the dish. Lay it on top of the fish mixture, generously brushed with melted butter, and cut with a sharp knife almost through the pastry, in a diamond pattern. Heat the oven to Gas Mark 6/400°F/200°C and bake just above the centre of the oven for 25–35 minutes, or until the pastry has risen and is a rich golden brown.

The Author

Josceline Dimbleby was born in Oxford in 1943. From the age of five her childhood was spent abroad, mostly in the Middle East and South America, so that at an early age she learned to appreciate a wide variety of food.

Josceline's instinct has always been to create her own recipes, which results in varied and interesting dishes, but leading a very busy life herself she appreciates the value of advance preparation and simple methods and most of her recipes reflect this view without in any way affecting their originality.

Josceline regularly writes cookery articles for the national press and has featured on television and radio. Her first cookery book, *A Taste of Dreams*, appeared in 1976, followed in 1977 by *Party Pieces*, a booklet for the Victoria and Albert Museum's Silver Jubilee Exhibition of Young British Craftsmen. The first of her series of cookbooks for Sainsbury's, *Cooking for Christmas*, was published in autumn 1978.

Josceline lives in London with her husband, journalist and broadcaster David Dimbleby, and their three children.